# Stranger

**Emily Hunt**

The Song Cave

The Song Cave
www.the-song-cave.com
Emily Hunt, 2023
Cover image: © Emily Hunt, 2023

Design and layout by Janet Evans-Scanlon



ISBN: 979-8-9878288-3-0
Library of Congress Cataloguing-in-Publication Data has been applied for.

FIRST PRINTING

# Contents

(I'm talking about the thing that stirs inside movements)
the way
the leaves of a plant are always more transparent at their edge
and its body slowly slowly from the center spreads

—ELENI VAKALO, "PLANT UPBRINGING,"
TRANSLATED BY KAREN EMMERICH

# I.

## Little Money

Fried at Whole Foods
I buy Laura flowers
Scan the cheap ones
And choose a better bunch
A lone green
Petal curls, a new rule
Deeper down
The poison lily, milky
Alive as ever
Holding water,
Stars, I love them leaning near
Held up there,
Royals
Absorbing food
I love to spend my money on a flower
Get sucked in
While she sleeps
Cut its yellow light with a knife
Feeling bigger
Slide it in
Among the others
I love to lie like this
Against the limit
Browsing the bright basement
To spend beyond
Cold and whole, to glide

Little on the elevator
Avoiding grime
Carrying them
Returning home
I fill a dimming room
With a flower when I enter
A sturdy one the sun
The little fuzz it has, lit
Dying like that
Any ageless day
But it's this one, slow,
Rootless as a cloud
And harder
Odd house
For the calico
Shoving her splotched head
Into new water
Her different beauty
Closing space in secret
I love to fake my freedom
So my balance shrinks
Like water drying
It's my revenge
Obviously
I love a flower in my face
Breathing past the shadows of its freakish traits

## Company

It’s rare to pull a bad bloom
straight from the mass
without breaking a stem
or losing a petal,
so we must cut
the band at the base
let it snap & then inch
the flawed flower out
preserving the shape.
We nudge another
into the bunch
at exactly the angle
that allows for the head
to face out and fill the hole.

*

By the second week
they are delivered pre-made.
A pallet of tall boxes arrives
at the square door
and the truck drives away.
We walk over with clippers.
We snip each white plastic strip
to release them from each other.
Often, two of us lean in
to cut the same one.

*

We break down the stack,
lowering six from the top
then dispersing the base.
We pull black plastic buckets
out of the boxes
and dump the water from each
into larger, sturdier buckets.
We pour this down
a slope of concrete
and the dark splash dries.
I often volunteer for this part,
as it allows me
to leave the group
for a minute or two,
to look into my phone
with my computer in mind.

*

A lack of air.
A gathering of thorns,
a limpness, a distance to close
a bent outlier unwilling
to lean or bounce toward
a more vacant center.

*

Before each arrangement's inspection
we must remove a cone of clear wrap
and dispose of it.
This thin stuff won't crunch
flat or into a ball.
It immediately reopens
and will often skid
down the side of the trash can,
sparking with static
rather than falling
fully into it.
It will hover near the top,
one of its sides
skating the rim,
until something solid
like a handful of stems
or the dropped head of a rose
pushes it down.

*

We pick off brown petals we spot
and toss them into large, green
compostable bags
lining trash bins
cinched to the rims
with giant rubber bands.

*

At the end of the line,
once they're wrapped and tied,
the pointed red roses
are hard and tight.

*

The bow drapes low
if the ribbon is long.
The pin at the knot
glides out once it's set.
We pull loose threads from the edges
where the woven cloth
made hard
by liquid starch
comes to a point
in support of the flowers.
We build hexagonal boxes,
bending their pre-creased sides,
and fill them with rows
of each kind of order,
tucking and forcing
the cool bundles
as close together as possible
to save space.
Then, we tug and release the door
to load the refrigerated truck.

*

A firm daisy too tall
for the tied crowd
hovers like a clown.

*

Flattened, twisted
toothpaste tubes
clashing on a dusty washcloth.
The white charger of a toothbrush
with a tiny head, plugged in.
I shower in the afternoon
when no one else is home,
my greasy phone on a ledge
past the curtain in steam.
Little sun leaks in.
There are shampoo bottles lined up
in staggered rows
on the chipped sill
left by those who lived here
last year, years before.
Some nearly empty,
blobs clogging their openings,
others closed and heavy.
The opaque ones you judge by their weight.
Under the shortest, strongest
streams to the scalp,
the taste of metal
slips in my washed mouth.
I imagine swirling them
into one pallid liquid.
The dregs of each kind
left to dry.
A patch of light

crosses my breathing eye,
hair darkened against me.
My limb dips
where the chased vein crosses
the warm blue, the only
living system I own.
Flushing I wish him dead.
Cloudy substance in hand.
I would then rinse and recycle the bottles.
They would go on to be part of some pile.
White plastic in soil.

*

The stripping the thorns,
the gripping the wet
garden gray gloves,
the forcing them down
sturdy thick stems,
the shaking off
wet wasted leaves
into the bin.
The reaching for pale
plastic from each
deep white container.
Thorns in the skin
at the edge of the nail.
The sweeping up clippings
and squeezing cold foam.
The cold folding the foam,
the dipping the mass
into a cup then a bag
from a stack.

*

Threads of burlap
float in my water glass
as I cram pebbles
into the spongy topsoil
of a potted succulent.
White wires to my ears,

I flick dirt off the blue rim.

*

I was told on the first day
standing with women
I had met moments before
I could rise, if I worked
hard on the flowers
to be "the cream at the top."
This was said not directly to me
but to all of us
gathered loosely around
a clean, silver table.
One woman could be promoted
said the Head of Production,
Sarah, the wife of one owner.

*

Holding out
a dewy bouquet
for the company's Instagram,
standing straight alongside
seven or so women
angling their arrangements
toward Sarah's
suited, centered husband,
some of them blowing
kisses or sticking their asses

out, bending down,
posing for an investor
visiting the warehouse,
beaming as I stiffen,
surrounded by scattered cool green
pieces of plants,
red clouded whiteboards,
and trash cans with wheels,
I'm aware of my role,
the other, sitting and sliding
within it, the friction
hotly melding the two,
the two turning
to four, the many million bodies
making this true.

*

I keep shifting the stems around
until the flowers face forward
and lie flat.
The thorns and knobs
bump into each other
and throw it all off.
The worst are the kumquats,
which fall to the floor
as soon as I add them.
It isn't natural
for a thin stem with fruits
to sprout up—

they're heavy,
they're supposed to just hang.
They scatter, get smashed
and stick to my shoes.
I eat one and taste the chemicals.
It's fine to swallow the skin.
At the end of the shift,
my broom sticks then skids
across the places they've been.

*

Before my interview
I signed an agreement
swearing apparently
to never disclose
procedural information,
policies, formulas,
any free detail
that could be caught
and then twisted,
repeated, construed,
when language came to be used
by competitors, customers,
dark horses, employees
let go or eager
newcomers to the game.

*

An iPad took my photo
as I leaned in to skim
the contract, barely caring,
wanting income and lunch.
I never saw it, but surely it's blurry,
my pupils streaks.
I'd probably like taking
a photo of this picture
of my face at work
and texting it to someone
who knows me.

*

On a mellow mobile shift
I work in a van
parked in a still neighborhood
near the beach
handwriting personal notes
from the system.
One says *I love you*
and is signed *Best,*
A few are written to semi-famous people.
There is often not enough room
on the pre-creased paper card
for all the customer has to say.
It is odd to read
brief sentences and phrases
addressed to the loved ones
of the sick or recently dead

and to Ashton Kutcher
alone in the van
with a view of the water,
to read and then write
*good luck, you rock,*
*see you tonight!*

*

Recycling containers
chock-full of bruised petals
wait in the warehouse
to be composted.
From far away,
they look perfect.
Huge, pretty piles.
Weightless red worlds.
Rich flakes of silk
that should never have been
torn from anything.

*

My mobile role allows for a trip
to the black-tiled bank
with Judy, a chatty employee
wearing a billowy t-shirt
printed with the company's first logo.
It's freeing to see her
laugh at her own jokes

in the driver's seat,
to run a simple errand
and break on the clock
the thorough silence
with someone who seems
at once content
to the core, and nervous.

*

When orders are placed
in the city, they suddenly appear
on my station's iPad
entering their spots
like ghosts on the list
categorized by neighborhood.
Certain drivers
take loaded boxes
to designated stretches
and quickly deliver
the bar-coded flowers.
The app tracks the action
as it happens.
For many hours
with striped stray ribbon,
blinking batteries,
extra labels, and scissors,
seated at a brand new folding table
in a barely used van,
I watch the lists change,

stepping out now and then
to look across the street
at pale, flat apartments
and the wild cold sea.

*

Feeding an infant for cash,
monitoring the tug of her new mouth
locked wet to rubber, her dark eyes
glossed, her few pounds rocking
in a remodeled dim
2-bedroom in the Mission,
my phone in my free hand,
I read that this company's
three founders copied
a similar, smaller company
launched years earlier
by one woman
who had the idea.
They were sued but settled it.

*

*Summary:*
*The Court concludes*
*that Farmgirl has failed*
*to carry its burden,*
*failed to satisfy*
*its burden of establishing*
*a likelihood that it will suffer*
*irreparable harm,*
*absent an injunction.*
*Given Farmgirl's failure*
*to shoulder its burden*

*to demonstrate a likelihood of success,*
*the Court at this juncture*
*need not reach*
*the balance of the equities*
*or the impact of any such injunction*
*on the public interest.*
*Farmgirl's Motion is DENIED.*
*IT IS SO ORDERED.*
*PRAYER FOR RELIEF:*
*Farmgirl Flowers prays*
*for judgment*
*against BloomThat*
*and for the following relief . . .*

*

When I come across flowers
at people's apartments
in cloudy water, or for sale
by the liquor store,
divided by type
into the same dinged buckets
we stack by the entrance
and roll on cold carts
to the trucks, I resist
picking them up
like they're mine.
Plucking bad petals from them.
Those that lean out
from the center

open to workers and wind
passing over,
as separate as they are attached,
gathered outside the lit interior,
wrapped in paper
and grown from thin air,
these are especially tempting.
The sound of the action,
this pull from the stalk
away from the style,
is nearly mute but
briefly satisfying.

*

One free succulent
needs no care.
It sits in a chipped container
deemed unfit for customers,
inches from a black candle
I rarely light.
It doesn't look dead,
just slightly puffy,
like there's water inside
ancient and it's green,
awake as an animal.
I don't know what makes a succulent thrive.
They look so resilient.
The owners added them to the menu
as "an option for men."

A stout blushing plant
depleted in certain air,
for men to receive, and to give.
I dig out the drowned wick.
It's me and the flame.

*

I have looked
in moments of distraction,
between tasks
or intentions, preceding
any momentum,
at Facebook photos
of each young owner.
A knee jutting out,
a sneaker pressed to a rock,
dry leaves covering the path
blurred behind them,
their teeth shining
in tropics and woods.

*

On certain days
I leave with a reject bouquet.
Yellow tulips, our staple.
Sweating on the bus
in long sleeves I've worn
for the cold warehouse
ignoring these stems,
their cupped heads
crossing my thighs,
I scroll through job listings
on websites I've memorized:
*constantly perform desk-based computer tasks*

*occasionally stand/walk, grasp lightly, use a telephone*
*rarely twist/bend/stoop/squat, kneel, crawl*

*

Because I'm immediately warm to him
at 7 a.m., my coworker
shows me an app to download.
Access to the radio in any country.
He says he never browses,
he always chooses a program
similar to that TV series
*Cheaters*, in which
the lies of boyfriends
and husbands are revealed live
as women are filmed crying
in dark, ecstatic relief,
finally found to have been
right all along,
their faces loud, damp
skin in flashing light.
Were women caught too?
I can't remember,
I watched it in elementary school.
I'm confusing it with *COPS*,
a "reality ride-along" that became
the longest running show on Fox
once *America's Most Wanted*
was canceled after 23 years.
I felt the ancient ugly

blur of a near-laugh
quickly withdrawn
when a *Cheaters* cop had curves,
long hair tied back,
the drawl of a girl at work,
and she turned the wheel
navigating with ease
a dim neighborhood of adults,
and she slammed on the brakes,
screeching the car to a halt.
Belt cinched at her waist,
the policeman then barged
into a stained, carpeted room
where no one expected her.
*Cheaters* airs on Saturday nights
and you can stream it forever.
I assume the plot
of the first episode
of the newest iteration
is essentially the same
as it is in every episode
of every brutal season
apart from the updated
graphic design,
a gold cracked heart
under a magnifying glass
that also serves as the C
in *Cheaters*, and falls like a rock
into place on screen

as the theme song
"Broken Hearted" strikes up—
*Cheating is a crime,*
*it happens every day*
*There are people running around,*
*soon they'll have to pay*—
and apart I assume
from the quality, the subtleties
of each core conversation
fueling, directing,
gauging the many
individuals involved—
their warm enemies and lovers,
their love run dry.
Instead I listen as I sweep
and prep the bruised, thirsty product
to Julianne Moore on *Fresh Air.*
Her exquisite life
floats unbelievable,
material, carried,
real and she delves in
soothed, soothingly, as if
lunching at the leafy edge
of the world's shadow,
relaxed as she reflects,
mildly touched
by its scope, nearly melting
with pleasure as she relays,
neutral as a stream,

a previous terror or stress
she refers to like a book
she's torn through
so casually with Terry, so clearly
she's conquered it, she's rich,
lives in New York at times LA
and she laughs at the thought
that her past pressed down
a metal plate on her breast
as she recounts
her child's little habits
in the bricks and foam of Greece.
The traveling sound
of two women competes
with the bad blaring music
my manager has chosen,
but I can still hear Terry,
a host so practiced at pulling out
the voice of a person flung far beyond
their mundane birth,
warmed by the memory
of being nobody,
brushing off the dirt.
To hear it at work,
a loosening distance,
small teeth in the memory,
biting the cloth net,
an occasional thorn
scratched against metal,

my hand hot from my phone,
I drag the cursor back
when I get distracted
by the percussive ads,
missing key parts,
telling pieces,
telling rampant stories
to my future as I fill
fifty-five budget cans
to which I've glued gold
floral paper
with dangling kumquats
and flowers, plastic-wrapped
food packs, and hot pink
anemones, their intricate centers
the dark triumphant ends
of long, fuzzy stems
cut with classic orange scissors
to similar lengths,
and as I deftly
band to them
limp green bags of water,
cool like toy organs,
for drinking in transit,
to ensure they will
survive a ride
on a truck loaded long ago
with heavy, organized
carts of crawling succulents.

## Delivery

There's something about a person
at home midday, receiving an order,
not hearing their voice from the van.
The tulips handed over,
silent, yellow and green,
leaving their long history
in the warehouse, the truck,
the dirt entirely.
The days when their young
stems were rooted
in rows, or waves,
deep, held and changing, not seeing
the customer's face, really,
a blur of hair or half an arm
as I wait outside their home,
holding my phone.
My coworker making her way
back to me, the only one
walking for miles,
the moving sea mute.
It's when I'm alone
in the white van
and I dip just briefly
back into my privacy
I feel most new to the city.

# Warehouse

Some of them I would get to know,
other names would never stick.
We would turn the days swiftly.
We would pick product up,
put scissors down.
Cut strips of ribbon or green foam—
we could choose and switch.
Working groups orbiting
flattened, stacked boxes,
ourselves in a way, we'd reenter
each duty, craving each end
of each quarter hour.
Strangers would want, buy,
eat, enjoy what we made,
when they reached for it,
and when they came across it.
They would start to love it, love getting it.
The knowledge that they wouldn't be living,
in the ways that they are.
It would just float, or take over.
I would sweat, feel cold, interested and young.

*

I worked faster to prove that I could,
slowed down, to sense myself move.

Escaping my manager's music,
I'd retreat to the toilet,
stare at the short rose on its back.
Flush the plain water, meet the mirror.
These small acts would have no effect.

*

A woman asked for a raise and got fired.
She was replaced by the end of the day.
Three men would arrive in the evening,
charged by the city.
They'd slide past us, up the stairs into glass offices.

*

New masses continued to seek what we fashioned.
They would either go looking
or they could not even bother.
Flattering images found their way to them,
via impressions.
Bulbous cookies, mandarins,
tight wreaths and blue flowers.
The arrangements we created would lean,
droop, and expand, out in the world,
overwrought, crammed together, but alive.
Their value would transform
over time, as word spread,
each climbing number thrilling the owners.
Rows of computers would be replaced,

clear plastic peeled from the backs
and smooth sides of the new ones.
They'd overheat, require updates.
Galaxies would glide over their screens.
Tasks would accelerate, roles would blur,
and procedures would shift.
We would keep up,
and people would begin to want more.
I might be one of them, working for you.

## Stranger

I dream of taking the baby out of the house.
Waking up, she registers
the edges of her crib
and the mobile above.
Her eyes like new leaves.
I microwave a white bowl of water.
She begins slowly to move
and I reach in to lift her.
I prepare her, changing her,
holding her warm, clean
flesh in place,
extending a free hand
for a flat, tiny hat,
unrolling a sock
onto each smooth foot.
I struggle for a while
to arrange her limbs
in the tangled cloth carrier.
She squirms on me in the mirror.
As her mini clothes spin
hot in the back room,
I pull the gate closed,
lifting it slightly
so the lock tongue lines up.
I share her with the block.
Metal chains and blue leaves

painted over a soaked couch in the street.
But what could be louder than her,
alive like a dog.
Heavy as a bag of food.
Her feet hang, her warm eyes
roll back. She bites my finger
with a soft, wet mouth.
Passing clean cars and thin trees,
their smooth bark
painted white at the base,
taking in the hard, layered leaves
of each potted succulent,
I consider calling someone familiar
as the baby looks up at me
and fixes her eyes there,
her weight buckled to mine,
her sock falling off.
I'm starting to get to know her.
She has a center.
I fear tripping over a branch
or discarded plank
and crushing her beneath me.
Wrong light, like bits of concrete,
where stars should be.

# II.

# Emily,

Do you believe it's possible
to be dominated
and respected
simultaneously?
I'm interested
in getting to know you better.
I felt endeared, repulsed
and bemused
viewing your photos.
I spend a lot of time
thinking about
tits, ass, what I'm going to be
when I grow up.
You should message me if
your lower body resembles
these buffalo wings I once ate
that were so plump and tender
they should have been wrapped
in sweatpants that say
Juicy on the back.
Girls often notice
my pecs, biceps,
symmetrical facial features
bone structure, crotch, etc.,
and guys, their feeling of envy.
I'm really good at

all. You should message me if
you like a man with a few rough edges
and won't secretly plot
to smooth them out the whole time.
Do you feel like you can write well?
For a white girl
you look like a decent rapper.
You look pretty gangsta
for a white girl.
Can I sleep with you?
It would really help.
I could never do without
water, it's so pure.
Do you love hot sex?
Hello there.
You have some very atypical pictures, hello.
Hey! You look like you like to have fun.
What are your days like?
I'm just hanging,
going swimming whether summer or winter,
taking trips to tropical places,
going out to eat.
I'm diligently striving
to live a life of true purpose
and trying to find
true purpose while I'm at it lol.
There's a grammar mistake
I your what am I doing
with my life section.

You could probably create
a killer erasure
if you were stuck in a cave
with all the food and water you needed.
I always love to see other people's
creative processes, so forgive me
for what I imagine will be
the start of a barrage of questions,
but what inspires you to write?
Who/what has influenced your style
and, I guess, to a further extent,
the principles that guide your writing?
I'm constantly making simple, overlapping
generalizations about life as a whole
in an attempt to actively examine
the world as I pass through it.
I'm always focused on something or another.
You should message me if
1. You're not shy
2. You like coffee
3. You've got a great personality
and you want me to know it.
My humor is dry as a dessert
but my moves are sleek as silk.
I love bad puns, cities, and life in general.
I was also on Jeopardy once, as a subject.
So, take that as you will.
I'm a huge Velvet Underground fan.
I saw Lou Reed live in 2007,

he played Femme Fatale,
and I was the only person in the audience
to sing along.
I could never do without thoughts,
Science, Kindle, Beaches,
Friends, Beer, The Atlantic,
The Economist, The Liberal Elitist, Skylines.
Honestly, I'm having troubles
putting my life into a confined box.
It tears at my values of being human.
Hi there!
I'm enjoying my life
through and through.
I'm a city person.
Good morning.
I just visited your profile.
I don't know you anything
special or important to say.
I'm a great guy if you get to know me
but mostly pissed off lol.
Ever been with
two European guys?
Would you be open
to an ongoing, casual relationship?
Your profile is very intriguing.
Artists are a dying breed it seems.
Welcome, stranger.
Have you ever used the word
dreamy to describe someone?

I used to live on a road
named after you.
It was a beautiful place
that Google maps couldn't find
where I could wander out into the yard
almost every afternoon.

## Native of Heaven

What if we had
a woman president
right here on the ground
in 2014.
Would they make jokes about her blood on *SNL*?
Or compare her shocking term
to the spacious cycle of a lily?
Would hate or pity win?
I guess I don't want to do it
but I would like
dental insurance.
I care about my skull.
What if when I got my check
it was a decent portion
of a full year's salary
marking with the strength of math
every hour I'd spent
teaching children how to read.
Every winter in our world
I could use that money
to pay for my heat.
So sheepishly
raised by the dead
and dying men
I might step into
high hot water

and wait for spring.
Even once it drained
there wouldn't be much
space for someone else.
Opaque in my periphery
might stand steadily
the shapes of houses, settled sky,
ice crystals, concrete
grains and flowers,
clean April wind,
and my leaders, so good
at shutting doors.
What if my kid grew up in this
a little dead between the categories?
Is it not strange that man—
with the pages of history spread out before him—
is so slow to admit
the intellectual power,
the moral heroism of woman,
and her identity with himself.
If we could first know where we are
we could then better judge
what to do, and how to do it.
It will become all one thing
or all the other.
Where is the broad and generous confidence
in the efficiency of true
democratic institutions?
You cannot deny one class
the full measure of their natural rights

without imposing restraints
upon your own liberty.
These things were said by
Elizabeth Cady Stanton, Abraham Lincoln,
and Carl something a century and a half ago.
Ten years later
Lincoln's long gone clamor
went wandering to claim that
the mystic chords of memory
stretching from every battlefield
and patriot grave, to every living heart
and hearthstone, all over this
broad land will yet swell
the chorus of the Union
when again touched, as surely they will be
by the better angels of our nature,
but I don't think it happened.
A few days ago
one of my students
argued against equal pay
while I stood in front of him.
The girl to his right
apologized after class
for being such an airhead.
When I was 14, this girl my age
was raped at school
and in the morning
they announced it.
She was called a liar and a dumb slut.
She transferred and I ran into her.

Maybe she'll be president.
It might be sort of like
how it is now
except we'd watch a woman's speech.

# Doritos

In 1937, Simone Weil experienced
ecstasy in an ugly church.

At 34, she was weak,
hungry, impossibly

bold, dead by '43.
Weil was really into the word

*supernatural.* She circles around it.
The ideas she is building

come back to it.
It ends many sentences

containing her
so she gives it a life.

*Man's great affliction*
*which begins with infancy*

*and accompanies him*
*till death, is that looking*

*and eating are two different*
*operations. Eternal*

*beatitude is a state*
*where to look is to eat.*

My chip was invented
after her time.

*Man only escapes*
*from the laws of the world*

*in lightning flashes.*
*It is through such instants*

*that he is capable*
*of the supernatural.*

I've watched a cat
eat a Dorito in grass,

have eaten whole bags
by the black sea.

They are plain, thin,
fried, dry

corn until they're covered
in bright powder.

*Salt, cheddar cheese,*
*maltrodextrin, whey,*

*monosodium glutamate,*
*buttermilk solids, romano,*

*whey protein concentrate,*
*onion powder, partially*

*hydrogenated soybean*
*and cottonseed oil,*

*corn flour, disodium*
*phosphate, lactose, natural*

*and artificial flavor, dextrose,*
*tomato powder, spices, lactic*

*acid, Yellow 6, Yellow 5,*
*Red 40, citric acid, sugar,*

*garlic powder, sodium*
*caseinate, disodium inosinate,*

*disodium guanylate, nonfat*
*milk solids, whey protein*

*isolate, corn syrup,*
but I want more of them.

*Contradiction is the point of the pyramid.*
*Doradito* means "little golden thing."

## TV

One man slides his hand
down the length of a counter.
He talks about his relationship,
concerned, agitated,
then he's silent.
Fruit sits in a bowl,
waxed, flawless and raw.
I like the character
because I feel more
inclined to behave like him
or decide that I have, in the past,
acted in comparable ways
when living with people.
By the end of the episode,
I prefer the woman's personality.
I like her especially
in the last scene
when she loses it,
stands up and leaves,
centering the hidden crew.
The sky changes,
but it's planned.
A truck pulls up with food,
like something new will happen.

# Houses, Your House

The telephone network
starts in your house.
A pair of copper wires
runs from a box at the road
to a bridge at your house.

From there, the red and green pair
connects to each phone.
If your place has two lines,
then two separate pairs
run from the road to your house.

The second is usually yellow
and black inside your house.

Sound waves from the voice
compress and decompress
the granules, changing their resistance
and modulating the current
flowing through the mic.

A thick cable will run
directly to the company
or it will run to a box
the size of a refrigerator
that acts as a concentrator,

digitizing your voice
at 8,000 samples per second,
then combining your voice
with dozens of others
to send them all down a single wire.

The division of a city
into small cells allows
extensive frequency reuse
across a location
so that millions of people
can speak simultaneously.

Any real phone contains
a coil or something
functionally equivalent
to block the sound
of your own voice
from reaching your ear.

# Landline

A phone was screwed
to the wall by the shower.

A clear one, with blue cords
so everything was visible.

The tangled system
of a single, labeled thing.

I thought: rows of them
coded, packed, stacks for sale.

Phones like sleeping backs in the dark.
How each current would twist

through the body of its device
snaking, tied to the others,

a fine line to the outlet,
and live hot inside the wires.

*

When I used it,
spine against the tile,

splayed limbs,
a skating eye on the grout,

he would listen in
from the floor below,

a smooth receiver to his ear
in a room he called his office,

where he browsed the internet
for hours in the sun.

He would at times
bark into the phone,

like a dog, or just breathe.
He could pick it up,

my voice, cut it off.
Could then refer to it, enraged,

or ignore it, like dry clay.
Feral in this way

he could not be disturbed
raking the morning

or the late afternoon,
taking, resting,

boiling, a human in his way.

*

Warm soil, I would call
to get the endless drone

of the busy signal.
Concrete, pavement,

dandelions and tires I would trace
the rough curve of the school

making my way
to the spare room phone

extra slow to join
each mild shadow

as if to sidestep
the result, to push

through and past, to trash
the minutes, seconds, flipping into deep

bland hours, pillowy and cruel.
I thought: I would return

and I would return
to the bright, basement level

vacant evening classroom
where 1688 was written

in long loops of chalk
marking the vast, flat

lawn of the display
cold under flies and lint

in the lights when it rained.
Battle on the board,

body for something.
My recent history

local and beating.
Related I could draw

a number or a word,
a dry, wood base

and dirt for the flower
I could erase.

Could write the date,
my ride elsewhere

deep in a computer,
his sense of time gone.

*

When he slept heavily
at the head of the table,

a man in a chair,
shut down

flickering and drowned, a body
with a plate in front of him,

I would cross
with a groundless warm gaze

his long lashes, each linked
floating face in the room,

the mound of my food,
I would think my way through

the unified
regions of the brain.

The things that happened
bled into the language we exchanged.

*

I imagine that now
the psychotic hold

phones in their beds
and naturally like magnets

they absorb
hundreds of videos,

short ones, a quarter way through
or several times in a row,

gliding past pausing,
going suddenly loud,

mute, these screens
may perk or spark

a kind of rest or yield
the opposite effect,

as any wet free walk
through the woods or trip

to the store can,
any glued green

photo of a pea,
real pea in a cold can.

*

Verizon, mygreatlakes.org
therealreal.com, Gmail,

my mother calls
as I'm approaching

the shallow stone steps
leading up to the Main Branch

of the San Francisco Public Library.
100 Larkin Street, cool sun,

wind, clearing itself of the day,
so steady it's unnoticeable.

Dry palm in its costume,
gold road leaning

toward a stuck tree.
Black leaves underneath.

Dirt below the buildings,
earth beneath the built dirt.

Hungry, my luck released
from the screen:

Marketing and Communications
Assistant. Digital Engagement

Associate Farm fruits dried
mud ghost prints on tight yellow tents,

and as we talk the market closes
down with pleasure.

She tells me my brother is in jail
for threatening to murder

my parents at dinner,
pushing them down

to the ground, reaching
like lightning

for a knife, cops and neighbors
staring, the moist air,

the moist eyes of strangers,
a narrowed glaring public:

Atlanta, ivy and dimmed
flaming maples at night.

*

They tried to call him in there.
Then, they learned the rule.

He would not be reached,
his body in action,

his body at rest in the cell.

*

When he faded
heavily across from me

a boy in a chair,
with a plate in front of him,

his hair growing close
to his food, his food going

nowhere I would look at
his long lashes

and think my startled way
through the separate

young and flashing
regions of the brain.

That soaked place, crossing
a wet, live

wire to the famous mind,
having made with mud

the skull, having held in class
the pale human

organ with yellow gloves
larger than my hands

having drawn
the whole eye:

sight, as if it had been sliced,
colored in the freest liquid space,

to learn the shape,
having labeled

the pupil, having thought
to exchange the view as if

hanging a coat
on a branch it bled into,

turning, to arrive
at a future, drawn and scrolling,

to exchange
my roots for some roaming

poem online,

## Freshmen

In college, a Mormon girl who lived on my hall
Asked me if I believed in God

I think it was late afternoon
I had that hollow in me still

No one had asked me before
I liked the question

We were walking on a white path
Behind the dorm, I said I sensed

A minding force,
Something in the air

Who knew us
Better, longer

Than we knew ourselves,
An exuding that would last

Wider, it existed first,
I never went to church

She was a virgin
Same here, when I met her

I was raped by Christmas break

*

The night before
He emailed me from the library

Was I in the library, the elevator
Opening to the basement

Rows of soft books to be shelved
And newer rows I remember

Walking up to those lights,
Switches you could flip

Cold grass into
The empty boy's bathroom

All white, many mirrors
Sharp, without borders

Nailed to the wall
At some point he had to have

Pulled the body
Into the stall:

Hate, wasn't I heavy

*

Days later, stars out, he messaged me on AIM
I was peeling an orange

Stout clementine with that easy pith, easy to lift, a rough leaf
Orange after orange, stranded

In bed below where I'd built
A grid of photos on the brick wall

Painted cream
I peeled back a plastic net

Stapled to the box of Cuties on my mini fridge
And reached for another, that first year of more

## Weekend Shifts

No dead leaves
so the city feels clean.
A gray dog trots by a man
passed out under a palm,
ruined by sun.
Cold bottles broken in the grass
touch the blue edge of a porta potty.
Clouds stretch and flatten
above Mission High,
silent and far from the smell.

*

The bookshop is pristine.
Wires from the dock
meet wires from each speaker
in a power strip
at the base of the scuffed wall.
I'm the one who cleans the single room
which grows larger as I use my minutes,
so I know where the rare filth sticks.
A pocket of air trapped
between my damp hair and neck
disperses when I pull it up,
twist it, and let it fall again.

A man walks into the empty store.
Speech.
Fluorescent light
sharp between us,
a row of stationary,
erasers in the shapes of pets,
a vintage book on knots.
He steps to the side
closest to my exit.
He leans on the counter,
his shoe near my backpack.
He tells me he's a director, spitting.
His teeth are the color of glue.
Trapped, I think of a dentist
paid to look inside his mouth.
I try looking through him
but he's loud.
Stiff second to second
I will him out,
roll my eyes as he leaves.
Drained, I straighten.
Minutes later, an unread email
surfaces in the store's static
info@ inbox. The name is random, but it's him:

> Emily,
> I want to open you up like an orchid and discover the actress you are,

I move through the store
spraying, wiping,
tightening displays,
pushing time forward,
thirty dollars in.
No one has bought anything.
Earlier, a woman walked in high
and signed the eNews list
with triangles and jagged lines.
She then circled the store, stealing gold pens.
Heavy light, somewhere in her things.
The entrance behind me
a hole to my back
open to passersby, as I looked
down the block at her hair.

*

I get off at 7, holding my phone.
A cloud above the register
follows me home.
I do see the saved voices in person.
They're part of my life.
The new ones, these versions.
One long and odd message.
I laughed at the end.
I left it by a chipped bench
with a view of San Francisco,
which happens to be right there
when I open my door.

*

I eat raw and packaged things
to avoid the kitchen's energy,
salami, a handful of baby lettuces,
a fat carrot from the drawer,
I can smell the soil,
sardines, spicy, silver
drenched in oil, two spines
down the drain and spoiling wine—

*

My weak computer,
two years older than my cell.
It overheats.
The cursor catches and delays.
Programs freeze and shut down.
Word is no longer supported.
iTunes doesn't sync with it.
Documents are sucked away.
When I write I can hear it,
people responding.
Traces of earth, a layer of noise.
The pace of my mother.
I wonder how it would be,
to divide sound with a machine.

*

I break off a corner of chocolate
wrapped in blue and green diamonds, clear text.
The creased paper lies open
beside my laptop,
dark bits melt
in the crevices.
I record my voice reading
and play it back.
A pair of scissors
sits on its shadow, touching a letter
from San Francisco General Hospital.
*This is not insurance*, it says in bold.
Holding my phone—
lithium mined from salt lakes
and hard-rock ore,
iron, copper, nickel,
tungsten, and tin, tiny
traces of silver and gold—
I post a photo of a poem
that includes my thumb.

*

Calmed by the locked door I read,

Flowers by the Sea

When over the flowery, sharp pasture's
edge, unseen, the salt ocean

lifts its form—chicory and daisies
tied, released, seem hardly flowers alone

but color and movement—or the shape
perhaps—of restlessness,

*

I slip a neon notebook
wrapped in plastic
into a paper bag
and give a guy his change.
Pages with no air between them.
My mood is light; bits of rock
and dust fall along
the rows of greeting cards
lining a steel shelf.
Over the next several hours
more will fall, so I'll let it gather
sitting relatively still
as the building's gutted
and the white smell of the wall's inside
grows stronger.
Once the slamming and shaking stops
I'll take all the cards off,
hold the sliding stack in my arms,
wipe each shelf in long strokes,
return them to their original order
and throw the blackened paper towel

into the street trash can.
I don't want to have to do it twice.

*

*Thank You, Congratulations!, Good Luck,*
the *Good* in red and a sun asleep—

> With thee, now freezing on thy slender stem.
> When once the heart-blooms by love's fervid breath
> Is left, and chilling snow is sifted in,
> It still may beat, but there is blast and death
> To all that blooming life that might have been.

*

My shift is almost over.
6 minutes left until 7.
The music will stop
when I close the app,
and I'll hear my steps more clearly.

*

I rotate the OPEN sign
and turn off the lights
as three cars inch toward the intersection,
shining and similar, like a family.

I see for the first time
across from the liquor store
a tree with a hole
cut from the dense mass of its branches
for the telephone wires to pass through.
The hole near me
like a hidden planet.
Its shape changes when I move,
white light collapsing into the leaves.
I pull down the security gate
and struggle to stick my tiny gold key
into the padlock
while holding my cracked phone.
I give in, putting it face down on the ground.
When my foot moves,
the phone shifts, grazing black gum
and my body rises as it does.

## Suicide

You hit raw dirt.
A dedication of sun,
your hand then
cold for hours.
Alone, a hunter
crossed you closed
your face, heavy,
arm firm across a root.
The image keeps me up
by the highway, rough
stranger, aged and cooled,
clothed son in dry leaves.
You were burned in a machine.

A few days in
I pull a dry towel,
blue but pale
from years of laundry.
Exposed in the colder corner
a large roach, its back slick
like candy but empty
untouched an inch
from the jug of bleach,
and the flowers are you.

You died in Pittsburgh.
*Erratic*, said the detective
who found your backpack wet,
miles from your body, a laptop
wrapped in wrinkled clothes
you'd worn to work, damp
from whenever it had rained.

*I think sometimes* you wrote,
*I'm in Hell*
*and being punished,*
*that everyone else*
*is an illusion—*
I called him back.
Which cop watched
a security camera's
footage of you
beside yourself
in a paved lot
searching 30 miles
from where you lived,
kicking a pile of sand in anguish
the final hour of your life?

There's this other video of you I have,
your young hair washed
blond in green light.
*It becomes what*
*the garden is really about—*
A photo of you new.

When I walk, I think of you walking
but it's more like falling—
my ribs against
the stone wall,
strong and building
the park's big body,
I look out at the city.
The bottom of a drained lake.
I'd pictured it before,
Manhattan, flatter
from its highest point
where it's farthest
even from itself, dusty
in January, asleep
like it's spending
this Monday with the dead.

A little manufactured
stack of napkins,
white in the wet leaves,
glass, ice, and the contact,
a coarseness, loose
little bits of bits of bits of rock.
Looking at the ground,
a thick tree breathing for me
is different now.
It's not that
you were never there.
Change, I love the air.

# Stuart's Sentences

Being alive is a good thing.
But I don't feel alive.
Sometimes, I feel dead.
I go and walk the street.
Sometimes I think I've lived
a long succession of lives on this planet
and that I am not young anymore
and it is good to think sometimes
I might be someplace better
in my next life. Sometimes I think
I'm in hell and being punished,
that everyone else is an illusion.
Sometimes I have these dreams.
*He spoke with God sometimes,*
*when he was stoned.*
Sometimes I think my father wants to throw me out.
*He could feel himself drifting*
*upwards, through the ceiling.*
That happened sometimes,
he'd found, when you inhaled
too much of the bitter smoke.
Sometimes, he listened
on his red and black headphones
to the song "Shimmer."
An odd, gnarled tree

stood next to him
against the high, stone wall,
like a corpse. He thought
this man might be
his father, glaring down at him.
But the corpse kept him company,
so Paul poured a drink for him onto the ground.
Sorry, I do that sometimes.
Sometimes I say some crazy shit.
Don't know why.
I told Laura that
I told Dr. Nichols there is a triad
of hero / victim / perpetrator
and I sometimes feel like all three.
I think we all are.
Our shouting made me realize
people other than me are suffering.
I am shocked by my capacity
to let my delusions make me
be cruel to people I love. I said,
because the barrier that separates
this world from the next
one is formed of something
immutable, we can never
understand ourselves any more
than we can understand why
the world is the way it is.
In effect you are longing
for something that is so fitting

to the human condition
that it is impossible to attain
/ not afraid of death. hey,
sorry about anything bad I've done
enjoy the mild weather

## Breakfast

Oatmeal with almonds, seeds, and cinnamon,
A hot sip, the region loud, red, a leaf in the Hudson,

Awake at the wrong time I transcribe
For $2 per audio minute

Quarantine

by Eavan Boland

The Poetry Foundation is posting it because she died:

*In the worst hour of ht e worst season*
*of the worst year of a whole people*
*a man set out from the workhouse with his wife.*
*He was walking—they were both walking—north.*

She was sick with famine fever and could not keep up.
He lifted her and put her on his back

# Tea

The door rings me awake, a package,
The guy's gone by the time I open it

Inside a box a bag of my grandfather's ties, printed with buds,
Stripes, the name of his college

Georgia Tech, my cousins finished
Clearing everything out of his house, same house

Where my mother learned
To eat, pee, read

## Farmer's Market

On gorgeous Halloween, first day in the 40s
Ginkgo unreal, totally new
Cones around a cavern
Where Broadway's bulldozed open,
I cross the street to avoid a psychotic veteran

## Frozen Sunshine*

There was that visit
To my brother, Easter 2000

Long weekend in the mental wing
Bringing him

That really pretty Sunday
A video of his dog, his only friend

Playing the tape
On the TV in the commons

Mounted by a square arm to the wall
A woman crawled toward my family

Barking like my dad did at home
Stuart stared blankly, upset

I'd made him a video,
He wanted his real pet

## Fiction Podcast

She read for the host
the voice of a person who'd died alone
in the middle of life, her body pulled
from the side of the road.
The clouds filled with blue air.
Half asleep on the highway
I heard from the back seat
her warm, current world,
her living lungs, a voice preserved online,
blasted into the car
as sound, I thought of yours,
so you could breathe,
or breathe through the lake,
a ray of dirty light.
Winter trees, damp at their cores,
shot through with sun,
they served as your shade, stripes
over your last minute's leaves,
their hidden roots crawling
through molten memory.
Wet spot where your thoughts went flat.
I didn't see you die near living deer,
look at you left in that way,
rippling out, cops in their moods,
the last to touch you in time,
lifted the body, slid it into the trunk,
and took you to your tone.

# Property

There are these flowers
with centers like liquid
and the outline
melts like a trick.
An illusion is usually
dark by the end.
An illusion is thin,
curving for some
spark, along it to trace
a straight
shot to the rigged
bones of the plot,
to drink the quiet dirt.

## Dusk

I don't get to walk around
Like I'm in the country
And only my own
Memory can see
Two bare feet, pale below the water line
Rounded to rock
Or the river's jewelry
Drying in the sun, sparkling
Past the mud
Don't get to wander young
In nothing else, in heat
Through snow
I don't get to go
Where that girl got murdered
In Morningside Park
A freshman, the deeper part
I forget her name
There's something there in her
I know it's near
Where nothing's going wrong
My body's covered
In one long butter-colored
Cotton dress stained with rain
I've just sprung up
In splashy sun
Of earth—a ghost pipe out of place

A corpse flower
The same temperature
As a human body
Giant as myself
Forgetting I am me
I get shoved, stood in front of
Called a cunt in the middle of the street
A pussy when I don't give you money
I'm stalked for blocks
By some smiling guy, skinny
And quite beautiful
Thin with liquid eyes
Sinister, in a tank top
I'd like to walk around at night
Or in the day, outside, where I live
With clothes I chose
The ones I've worn
Today, the jeans I have on now,
They smell like me, restless laundry
Too tight where I keep changing
I'd take my loop
Up the hill
To the church
The warmth of mourners mixing
Human myth, three purple stars
Scotch-taped to the windows
Cut from paled paper
Years ago by children, the faded rainbow
That would lift me
Those grown children's clouds

Creased closer to the endless stairs
I climb to get my groceries
Normal as those
Little white
Perfectly cut
Tags on city trees—
I'm Your New Tree:
At sunrise I'll get to see
That knee-high jail of all my favorite sky-blue weeds

# Love

Fruit in the sun
That could be us
Sun on fruit

## Canned Food

She sucks on my shirt
Kneading my ribs
A claw hooks a breast and I let her

Plump black duck
Sweet spring cow
She sighs just like a person does

My hair over her ear, love,
It's how she falls asleep

Four years bonded
To my body but no milk

Her brother licks
An Ikea plate, his tiny tongue
Across crusted bits

Hardened around
Fresh factory food
Pulp of murdered birds

Plops, I gag and smile, it's easy
Easier than anything
To hook my thumb

Pop and peel the top, drop the meat
The plate scrapes against the wood floor
And I give him more

# Indoor Cat

He was found on King's Highway, eating trash

I spray him to train him
but he vomits the leaves

or in the morning there's just spit
dried puddles by the outlet

His sister once vomited on a framed photo of us
It was hard to clean the corner

where the wet bits of it
soaked into the wood

so deep past the surface
it'll always hold the scent

The next day he licked it

## Owner

At the top of a hill each morning,
I wait for the bus by the donut store.
Its pink sign looks hot,
curls, like a rope.
You turn toward a jade
at the height of your neighborhood,
stop at a light, a steep drop ahead.
The sun starts to seep up,
reaching all grasses and grooves of the city.
A white bus with black windows passes.
A few minutes later, the city bus arrives like a room.
It crawls warm and dull to the east edge,
breathing its heat, a few baby hands
warming wide glass.
There's a phone number printed across
the billboard at my stop.
A man walks his sniffing dog below it,
sharp legs brushing wild onion.
At the base of the hill,
I enter my code,
push the gray gate open,
allow the worn loop of my bag
down my arm, walk to my station.
I drop the metal end of a hose
into a bucket, turn the tough faucet.
Traveling after the sound,

the cold rushes out
full force from the rubber,
breaking into itself, interrupting and filling
the round plastic space.
Hungry, I pick up the water.

## Trees

Our father's not yet dead.
His brother died alone in a hospital
Choking on a sandwich.
Bread, cold ham, mayonnaise,
Iceberg in an extra clean room.
Their father fought in World War II.
Maybe a nurse used a blanket
To cover the kid, at night
It might be his pain
I own, my uncle, that son
Who kisses my hair.
I think my grandfather was in the war.
His firstborn son's son
Died alone in the woods outside
Pittsburgh, Pennsylvania.
He was my sibling
So he jumped from a highway overpass.
When he was 15, he wrestled at 103.
That same small three moves on me.
It was hard to feel him lose,
To watch from the stands
As a strong tiny teen
Pinned him down and made him bleed,
Then shook his hand.
Once nature, a vacuum
Stole him from the future—

Once he was sick, his pills doubled his weight.
He wrote on his bedroom wall
With his blood: *Is this what you want?*
He slept in the basement, growing away,
Day after day, a pile of clothes,
Fungus, warm and mysterious
As my own changing brain,
Once I'd sunk into the soft place
Time gave me to die. At breakfast,
On Christmas, into silence, our father said,
*We could uh, hang the cat and watch him bleed.*
It's on a DVD my mother mailed to me.
I lived in Oakland, California then.
My sublet smelled like eucalyptus oil
I'd bought on Mission Street,
And the dried kind animal sweat
Of Lola, my roommate's rescue dog,
Who felt most at ease
When I lay flat on the rug.
My twin must be recording.
After he says it, no one says anything.
Blue bowls of blueberries, bacon strips
Lined up on paper towels
Translucent with grease,
Boxed Minute Maid, bright orange,
Poured into a pitcher near my dad.
My head in my mother's lap,
I'm pretending I'm asleep.
It's a beautiful scene—
In the '60s our father's brother,

Douglas Hunt, who I never met
Died as a teen. I met Doug's dad
Once, a year or so before
He died of cancer, my grandfather.
I was 2, there was muck on the pond,
Green, and the geese,
Guy's hand on my back.
My grandmother's son, blacked out,
Smoking, muttering to no one,
Kicked the cat
The second she stepped into the kitchen.
Ethical. No funeral,
As far as I know,
My dad's mom died alone.
Just a little yellow hair left
In an elderly care facility in Newton.
Autumn floating under the largest branch.
There was no funeral or flight
To bury the body.
Maybe she was burned but not scattered.
Finally, my father was
The last person alive
In his family. I was the last
Blood relative to see her, she kept saying
She remembered me
As a child, *your little brown shoes.*

# Notes

The epigraph is from "Plant Upbringing" in *Before Lyricism* by Eleni Vakalo, translated by Karen Emmerich (Ugly Duckling Presse, Lost Literature Series, 2017), page 26.

"Company" responds in part to working for minimum wage (on an assembly line and in a delivery van) in 2015 for BloomThat, an iPhone app-based flower delivery startup in San Francisco. Italicized phrases are pulled from an online record of a lawsuit filed against the company by Farmgirl Flowers, and from job listings on Indeed.com.

"Emily," is built from messages and profile excerpts found and received on OkCupid and Tinder in 2015.

The title "Native of Heaven" is a phrase lifted from *Paradise Lost*, Book V by John Milton. This poem includes phrases from the following speeches:

> Elizabeth Cady Stanton's speech at the Seneca Falls Convention at the Wesleyan Chapel in Seneca Falls, New York on July 19, 1848.
>
> Abraham Lincoln's House Divided Speech, delivered to 1,000 delegates in Springfield, Illinois after he had accepted

the Illinois Republican Party's nomination as that state's US senator, on June 16, 1858.

Carl Schurz's "True Americanism," delivered in Faneuil Hall in Boston, Massachusetts on April 18, 1859.

"Doritos" includes excerpted sentences (presented in italics) from *Gravity and Grace* by Simone Weil.

"Houses, Your House" is built from phrases found in *TCP/IP and Distributed System* by Vivek Acharya, published in 2008 by Firewall Media, publisher of computer Science & IT books for the educational and professional market.

"Weekend Shifts" includes an excerpt from "Flowers by the Sea" by William Carlos Williams and an excerpt from "A January Dandelion" by George Marion McClellan.

"Stuart's Sentences" is composed of sentences pulled from emails, stories, and essays written by my brother, Stuart Hunt (1982-2019). The diction, syntax, and phrasing of each sentence is preserved; I sequenced them and applied line breaks.

"Breakfast" includes the first six lines of "Quarantine" by Eavan Boland. Italics and the typo "h te" are mine.

The title "Frozen Sunshine" is a phrase lifted from "November 22" in *Diaries of Exile* by Yannis Ritsos, translated from the Greek by Karen Emmerich and Edmund Keeley (Archipelago Books, 2012).

# Acknowledgments

Poems included have previously appeared (sometimes in different versions) in the chapbook *Company* (The Song Cave, 2019), and in *Annulet*, *Folder*, *Hyperallergic*, *The Volta*, *Court Green*, *Tupelo Quarterly*, *jubilat*, Poets.org's Poem-a-Day series, the Poetry Foundation's PoetryNow series, *The Ocean State Review*, *Jerry*, *Hobart*, *The Spectacle*, *Totokaelo Editorial*, and *Harp & Altar*. I am grateful to the editors of these publications.

Big thanks to Ben Estes and Alan Felsenthal, two of my favorite artists in every sense.

Thank you, Claudia Rankine, for selecting a manuscript version of *Stranger* as an honorable mention in the 2020 Donald Hall Prize for Poetry competition. Thanks to the Kimmel Harding Nelson Center for providing time to read *Gravity and Grace*, and to the Vermont Studio Center for a room to write "Landline." Thank you, Nick Sarno and Paulina Nassar, owners of Press, for hiring me for a peaceful retail job with a healthy hourly rate; I wrote the first few stanzas of "Company" in your beautiful store in San Francisco. Thank you to participants in my poetry courses for many sparkly and nourishing hours on Zoom.

Major gratitude to Hannah Brooks-Motl, Dan Bevacqua, Georgie Devereux, Alexis Almeida, Jae Yeun Choi, Michele Christle, Shannon Burns, Jacob Otting, Laura Hunt, Sam Douglas, Karen Cumbus, James Kaplan, Aaron Kaplan, and Avery Kaplan for essential conversations, warmth, sustenance, and fun.

Stuart, I remember you. Thank you for putting your struggle into words.

Gigi and Miss Kiss, my animal family, you are so smart and cute! Thank you, Lina Makdisi, for bringing these creatures into my life.

Thank you, Dr. Amy Fowler.

Thank you, plants, sun, soil, air, and water.

Jacob and Saskia, wow. I love you. Thank you for everything, forever.

## OTHER TITLES FROM THE SONG CAVE:

1. *A Dark Dreambox of Another Kind* by **Alfred Starr Hamilton**
2. *My Enemies* by **Jane Gregory**
3. *Rude Woods* by **Nate Klug**
4. *Georges Braque and Others* by **Trevor Winkfield**
5. *The Living Method* by **Sara Nicholson**
6. *Splash State* by **Todd Colby**
7. *Essay Stanzas* by **Thomas Meyer**
8. *Illustrated Games of Patience* by **Ben Estes**
9. *Dark Green* by **Emily Hunt**
10. *Honest James* by **Christian Schlegel**
11. *M* by **Hannah Brooks-Motl**
12. *What the Lyric Is* by **Sara Nicholson**
13. *The Hermit* by **Lucy Ives**
14. *The Orchid Stories* by **Kenward Elmslie**
15. *Do Not Be a Gentleman When You Say Goodnight* by **Mitch Sisskind**
16. *HAIRDO* by **Rachel B. Glaser**
17. *Motor Maids across the Continent* by **Ron Padgett**
18. *Songs for Schizoid Siblings* by **Lionel Ziprin**
19. *Professionals of Hope: The Selected Writings of* **Subcomandante Marcos**
20. *Fort Not* by **Emily Skillings**
21. *Riddles, Etc.* by **Geoffrey Hilsabeck**
22. *CHARAS: The Improbable Dome Builders* by **Syeus Mottel** (Co-published with Pioneer Works)
23. *YEAH NO* by **Jane Gregory**

24. *Nioque of the Early-Spring* by **Francis Ponge**

25. *Smudgy and Lossy* by **John Myers**

26. *The Desert* by **Brandon Shimoda**

27. *Scardanelli* by **Friederike Mayröcker**

28. *The Alley of Fireflies and Other Stories* by **Raymond Roussel**

29. *CHANGES: Notes on Choreography* by **Merce Cunningham** (Co-published with the Merce Cunningham Trust)

30. *My Mother Laughs* by **Chantal Akerman**

31. *Earth* by **Hannah Brooks-Motl**

32. *Everything and Other Poems* by **Charles North**

33. *Paper Bells* by **Phan Nhiên Hạo**

34. *Photographs: Together & Alone* by **Karlheinz Weinberger**

35. *A Better Place Is Hard to Find* by **Aaron Fagan**

36. *Rough Song* by **Blanca Varela**

37. *In the Same Light: 200 Poems for Our Century From the Migrants & Exiles of the Tang Dynasty,* translated by **Wong May**

38. *On the Mesa: An Anthology of Bolinas Writing (50th Anniversary Edition),* edited by **Ben Estes and Joel Weishaus**

39. *Listen My Friend, This Is the Dream I Dreamed Last Night* by **Cody-Rose Clevidence**

40. *Poetries* by **Georges Schehadé**

41. *Wings in Time* by **Callie Garnett**

42. *Two Murals* by **Jesús Castillo**

43. *Punks: New & Selected Poems* by **John Keene**

44. *ABC Moonlight* by **Ben Estes**

45. *Star Lake* by **Arda Collins**

46. *The Maybe-Bird* by **Jennifer Elise Foerster**

47. *Seriously Well* by **Helge Torvund**

48. *Dereliction* by **Gabrielle Octavia Rucker**

49. *Bookworm: Conversations with* **Michael Silverblatt**

50. *April* by **Sara Nicholson**

51. *Valley of the Many-Colored Grasses* by **Ronald Johnson**

52. *The Sphinx and the Milky Way: Selections from the Notebooks of* **Charles Burchfield**

53. *Telling the Truth as It Comes Up: Selected Talks & Essays 1991-2018* by **Alice Notley**

54. *Lunar Solo: Selected Poems* by **Jules Laforgue**